Greece

Varasova

Stephen and Scharlie Platt

www.leveretpublishing.com

Greece: Varasova
First published - April 2018
Published by
Leveret Publishing
56 Covent Garden, Cambridge, CB1 2HR, UK

Corinthian bronze helmet, Olympia Museum

ISBN 978-1-9124602-1-2

Greece

Varasova

Greece 2003

Varasova
Nafpaktos
Patras
ATHENS
Arakynthos
Gavalou
Stamná
Makryneia
Gouriá
5
Aitoliko
Katokhi
Iera Polis Mesolongiou
Mesolóngion
Nafpaktos
48
Galatás
Varasova
Antirrio
alkan Peninsula
Patraïkós Gulf
Patras
Elikistra

Introduction

Varasova is a limestone mountain rising to 917m in south-west Greece 3 km east of Galatas, 14 km east of Missolonghi and 18 km northwest of Patras. It was known as Chalcis in antiquity, and there was an ancient Aetolian town at its foot. It rises steeply from the coast of the Gulf of Patras to 917 m elevation. There are rock climbing routes on the steep south and southwest faces of the mountain. Its south and southwest faces form an impressive promontory the end of which drops directly into the sea. Greek climbing began here in 1958, so Varasova has a special significance for Greek climbers and is one of the most popular cliffs in the country. Varasova is mainly a weekend venue, so mid-week it is usually deserted.

Varasova is approximately 4 hrs by car from Athens and with Meteora is among the best climbing areas in Greece. It is ideal for autumn climbing between September and November and the rock is very solid, relatively sharp and unpolished, and mostly gray or yellow limestone of outstanding quality. There is a great variety of routes: big walls, steep slabs, corners and vertical

Varosova mountain

cracks, flakes and hidden holds which make for sublime climbing over a translucent blue sea. The approximately 200 routes of Varasova include short and multi-pitch sport routes and several mixed routes with as many as 18 pitches that require traditional gear. Most anchors are bolted and set up for rappelling. There is still huge potential for new routes. Grades range from easy to very hard, the majority being in the mid-grades (5c-6b).

The mountainous region of Varasova has been declared as a historical area of outstanding natural beauty. The churches, monasteries and hermitages of the Byzantine era that were developed in the hard to reach slopes of Vararova today are all abandoned. On a low hill near the village of kato Vasiliki, south-east of Varasova there are the ruins of a Byzantine church dedicated to Agios Dimitrios dated from 11th century of great architectural interest. And on the south side of Varasova about 80 meters above the sea a wide rock shelter cave opens up in which are ruins of a byzantine eremite group dedicated to Saint Nicholas. Cave hermitages also exist in many other places in Varasova.

Varosova and Krioniri

Journey

Saturday 24 October

We travelled by train from Cambridge arriving at Ladywell in the evening and were met by Rose, an old climbing friend from days in the Cambridge Mountaineering and Caving Club. We collected a take-away curry as Rose been to the zoo and the circus with her boys, Robert and Paul, and had run out of time to cook.

Sunday 25 October

The alarm went at 4:30 and, despite having woken twice in the short night, felt surprisingly fresh. A friendly Nigerian drove us through London in the dawn, passing the canons of the Imperial War Museum and arriving at Heathrow in less than an hour. We had two hours before the flight left, which Scharlie regretted losing sleep but is happy that our flight path took us over the Alps and the sharp shadows and bright light gave us a clear view of endless

Corinth Canal

snowy ridges with the Matterhorn standing out unmistakably.

We flew from to Athens, hire cars at the airport and made a quick getaway, driving in convoy on motorway to Varasova via Corinth and Patras. The Gulf of Corinth flashed past so quickly it seemed like a deep ditch with smooth sides cut like a brown cheese. We stopped for bean soup in ancient Corinth then on, keeping up with Muny's erratic driving till we reached the ferry at Patras. There was some confusion because we were supposed to drive onto the ferry backwards, but didn't, and were shouted at by several traffic directors at once.

We had lunch in Corinth and a fish supper here in Krioneri, the hamlet at the foot of the crag. We installed ourselves in the flat and went out to the balcony to take the air. Rose said I think you can see the crag from here. She was right – we can see the cliff by the streetlights of the village it looked as large as a cloud blocking out the stars; huge and intimidating. Muny's list, which we studied in the restaurant, shows routes of eight pitches. Good job we went on the mini rocks behind Leveret Croft a couple of times before we came!

Ferry from Paktos across Gulf of Corinth (Now there is a bridge)

Monday 26 October

We went climbing today. The day dawned fine but by the time we set off walking to the crag it had clouded over. Scharlie had woken several times in the night so she hugged the blanket as long as possible. Muny was awake by 6am and drove us into town of Galata. The cafe was open for coffee but the shop for provisions not till 8:30am.

We set off at 9 and had only a five minute walk to the bottom of the crag along the beach road at the bottom of the crags, past climbers just emerging from their tents, heading for the slabs at the right hand end of the rocks. There are bolted sports routes and we climbed a ramp to the start. Although it is huge and intimidating the rock is firm and full of holes like Gruyere cheese.

Rose climbed with Neil while Steve and Scharlie went with Muny, starting on a sports climb of three pitches The names were marked on the rocks but we still don't know the Greek alphabet so couldn't read the name of our chosen route until Muny translated it as *Relax*. Muny asked Steve if he would like to lead so he tied on the top of the rope and set off. The limestone is very sharp and there are lots of holds. He got up the first pitch without too much difficulty and brought up Scharlie and then Muny, who led the next pitch.

Muny following Stéve on 'Relax'

Lots more Greek climbers began to arrive, quite a few coming to our area of the crag, which seems to be used as a training area. There was also a party on the steeper rock to our left. The final pitch of our route was a little harder but Steve finally reach the big ledge where Rose and Neil are coiling up their ropes having finished their route. Rose and Neil traversed off directly but Muny thought we should try higher so we climbed up to join the main way-marked path. It seemed much further going down and more precipitous.

Our route had had the desired effect in relaxing us, so Muny decided we should go onto the main face and do something harder called Skoupa. He

Steve belaying

wanted to try a longer route on the wall overlooking our apartment, so we packed the sacks and headed back round to the main cliff. We passed other climbers, some on what looked quite hard climbs, and scrambled up through prickly scrub to the base of the rocks. Muny found the route he wanted to try and, having geared up, set off. He took quite a while on a grey wall about two-thirds of the way and so we figured it must be hard. Proceedings were enlivened by a party of young Greeks who kept shouting Orfeo from the rocks. Orfeo proved to be the beautiful labrador who was swimming far out into the sea.

Rose braves the waters

Scharlie went next and managed it fine. When Steve came up he found Muny had taken so long because he had been fiddling small nuts into cracks to protect the moves rightwards around the corner. Moving up carefully on small footholds you found you could reach good handfuls and it wasn't too hard.

The weather looked threatening; the sky was dark and we could see rain to the east and lines of showers out in the gulf. Muny said the next five or six pitches were harder and there might be some route finding difficulty and that because we'd started late we should go down. Scharlie was relieved as she

Muny traversing round

hadn't liked the exposure. So we fixed a rope using one of Steve's tapes so we could be sure that the ropes would run and abseiled down the big, red, quarried wall to the right of the crack line we had been following.

By the time we got down the weather had improved and Muny wanted to try another climb, so we moved left to another larger crack line and soloed up a slanting chimney. Scharlie decided not to try this one and sat watching us.

When it's steepened Muny stopped and set up a belay. It was Steve's turn to lead, so he made a start. The chimney was easy at first but became more

Steve on Alkistis

Steve and Neil reaching top

bush, having put a runner round it and approached a steeper section. He was more worried now about running out of rope before finding a belay because the next section looked long and hard. He put in a friend and contemplated descending but pressed on and found two pegs, safeguarding the obvious small belay, clicked in and brought Muny up.

By the time he arrived it was spotting with rain. Scharlie had met the two Greek climbers who had been on the big wall to our left doing Afrikana. They asked her if we were experienced, since our route was very long and the abseil hard to find and it was raining heavily. She said we were and they commented that the English must be used to climbing in the rain. Muny asked Steve what he wanted to do and he said go down. Muny agreed, although he had obviously wanted to try the next harder pitch. Scharlie set off home and got back to the flat just as it started to pour. She could see Steve and Muny abseiling. They got down safely and mercifully the ropes pulled through and we packed up our wet gear and set off back to the apartment to be greeted from the balcony by Scharlie, Rose and Neil.

The toilet still wasn't fixed but Rose had commandeered a garden bucket to use for flushing and we managed to get a bath of tepid water by running the hot shower. So we felt quite civilised when we set off shopping in Galatas. We

General view of the slabs

spent some time looking for a guidebook recommended restaurant that was supposed to be opposite the church. It was no longer there, but we found a grill run by a Filipino lady and her Greek husband. She was anxious to impress and kept offering extras for free. This is the first time for a long time anyone who isn't Greek has been here, she said. All they are interested in is grills. We promised to return.

Tuesday 27 October

We woke after a good night's sleep and Muny suggested Scharlie and I climb together while he and Neil and Rose went to do the first route we tried yesterday.

We got a leisurely start and went round to the slabs again and this time chose a route called Hera – the widow. Scharlie said she'd like to try leading and so she started on the first pitch. She got as far as the steep wall that guarded the upper slabs and got a nut in that allowed her to move up safely and clip into the peg and lower off. But about 40 feet up she hit a difficult wall and decided to come down. Steve led after that and the climbing said he thought it was hard; the moves above the peg needed careful footwork

Scharlie with the friendly Alsatian

and patience to find good handholds. The second pitch was easier, although there was no in situ protection. There were abseil bolts at the top of the second pitch and clearly people didn't often do the final pitch, which looked intimidating; a reddish wall with overhangs at the top. It looked loose, but we tried it anyway and, in the event, it was quite pleasant.

From there we soloed. Unfortunately, descending a short wall a foothold broke off and Steve slipped. He held himself but banged his knee. Because his trousers were untorn he thought it was okay but moments later we saw his trousers were soaked in blood. It was very hot so we bathed the knee and the trousers in the sea, put on shorts and sat in the shade to eat lunch and watch Orfeo's party practising on training climbs which they were top roping We hung the trousers to dry in the sun while we had lunch in the shade then forgot to collect them when we went off to do another climb.

We decided to go to the right-hand end of the cliff and were seduced by a line of bolts but the climb proved to be easy so we abseiled back down and traversed further right above the sea until we found a route called Alkistis. It was one steep continuous pitch nearly 50 m. Scharlie said she had to concentrate hard to stay in balance, keeping breathing regularly and not

Scharlie with her adopted friend

looking down. The route was thinner than any of the other slab routes and a little steeper, but the protection was good and we pressed on to the top and abseiled off. The friendly Alsatian dog from our flat came with us and lay on the soft bed of ribbon seaweed waiting for us while we climbed.

The sunset over the sea was warm orange and blue and we spotted Muny and company high on the cliff face on Skupa, the route we tried yesterday. It was obvious they wouldn't finish the climb before dark. We saw their head torches flashing a few times but decided they weren't signalling. It was nearly

Scharlie abseiling

dark and they still had two more pitches to reach the top. We were worried for them but there was nothing we could do. Then we found we'd forgotten Steve trousers on the beach and went to retrieve them and found they'd gone.

Between making tea and having a bath we kept watch and finally saw their head torches on the top. We figured they would try walking down to the right as far as they could and then they might bivi. We felt warm and relieved it

Rose climbing

wasn't us. The earliest we thought they'd make it back would be 10pm so we went out to eat at the Capitain, the place we've been to on the first night. We were reading the guide having returned from the restaurant when we heard thumping at the stairs and the doorbell and it was them. They had found a path with red dots which led to the descent and found the abseil point in the dark. In three abseils they were down the sheer cliff face. It was impressive that they'd made it.

Statue of Byron dressed as a Turk, Missolonghi

Wednesday 28 October

Scharlie and Rose decided they didn't want to climb. Rose was keen to visit Byron's monument in Missolongi, where he'd died of a chill. Steve had to decide whether to go with them and have an easy day or go with Muny and Neil. He procrastinated for a while and then decided to have a day off. He regretted the decision later because Missolongi proved to be a boring and non-descript gridiron of a town.

Statue of Cervantes, Nafpaktos

We drove around for a while, criss-crossing the town, trying to find real centre without much success, so parked and walked. Rose followed her nose in what proved to be the opposite direction to the one we should have taken. Finally we asked in a chemist and he directed as to the Garden of Heroes near where we had entered the town. Byron's statue showed him dressed as a Turk with scimitar and crossed arms. It dated from 1995 so maybe there had been an earlier statue. We also tried the museum but it was closed. Cutting our losses we had a coffee in a nice cafe and used the facilities, then headed back for the car.

Rose thought she knew the way but again we went in the opposite direction to the one we should have and we had to retrace our steps. Later she admitted she had a tendency to follow her nose at random in strahge cities. Since it started to rain, rather than go back and walk on the mountain as we'd planned, we decided to go east to Nafpaktos, which Tony had recommended when we saw him in Athens. It was the site of the Battle of Lepanto in 1571, fought out in the bay between the caravels of the Genovese, Venetians and Spanish against the galleys of the Ottomans. Cervantes was reputed to have lost his hand in the battle. Nafpaktos is a much prettier town than Missolongi. There is a tiny port, reminiscent of a Cornish harbour, surrounded by cafes.

Nafpaktos

But like Missolongi there was little evidence of tourism and the restaurants and tavernas seem to be directing their efforts to attracting local trade. We clambered along the battlements and photographed ourselves with Cervantes, whose quill pen and sword were both bent. Again the statue was recent – maybe an EU project since there were a number of marble plaques referring to various official bodies in Madrid and La Mancha.

We had another coffee in an elegant restaurant and Rose and Scharlie had pudding and cake. On the way out we saw a sign to the castle on the hill, and decided to visit. There had been a Greek citadel on the site in antiquity, but

Scharlie

the fortress is Venetian. There is a tiny Greek church on the top and, trustingly, the door was open and the icons on display. It poured with rain on the way back so we were glad we weren't climbing. We got back just after Muny and Neil who had managed a good climb despite the rain and returned to the fish restaurant for supper. The proprietors were kind and courteous and a young women took Scharlie's postcards and said don't worry I will post them.

Thursday 29 October

It rained heavily in the night; long slanting rain which drums and pounds on the roof. This morning it's raining still and our faithful hound was wetly waiting for us and we wondered if he would venture forth today. This could be the end of the climbing since the women in the supermarket said it would rain the rest of the week. The rain abated at 11, however, and we ventured forth and tried our luck on the slabs, knowing that the friction was good and it would dry quickly. Muny offered to climb with Rose and Scharlie and I went to climb with Neil. Although the rain had stopped, Scharlie decided it would be easier if she sat it out, so Neil and I traversed round to the ridge and I led off on a very long easy pitch. We abseiled down and I suggested Neal led Alkista, that

Main Wall Varasova

Scharlie and I had done before. I enjoyed seconding it and realised I must have been climbing well when I'd led it.

While we had been climbing Scharlie went swimming. Although the sea was rougher than it had been on Monday when we'd watched the dog Orfeo swimming, it was still clear. She swam out into the bay so she could see us better. We could see her making languid strokes and swimming round the point. Later she said it was warm round her legs but icy currents from the river curled around her chest and arms. She loved it and it made her feel young and alive.

We changed partners. Muny and Steve climbed Hera again to retrieve the ropes that he and Rose had got jammed. But unfortunately, although we

Settin off on the first pitch of 'Bow'

managed to retrieve Rose's rope, we were unable to get our own ropes down. So while Muny went to get his bathing gear Steve climbed Anastasia to retrieve the ropes. Anastasia was different in that there was little protection and the moves were fairly undifferentiated. We got to the top and Neil retrieved the trapped ropes while Steve set up another belay. So despite thinking the day was a write-off we managed quite a lot of climbing retrieving stuck ropes.

Dinner at the Grill again. Florence had put on a special spread for us and even lit the fire. We could barely walk we were so full.

Friday 30 October

The weather was fine and Muny suggested Steve might climb with him and that we could try Bow again, the climb we had tried on day one. Scharlie said she wanted to try and walk to the top of the mountain, which would allow us to climb in a rope of two. I was concerned about Scharlie going alone; if she twisted her ankle she'd have difficulty getting down. But I showed her how to use my mobile phone and stressed she should only go on if she was sure of the way.

Muny and I set off for the crack, following a different better path that took us away from the crag so we had to traverse back through the thorn scrub. We left the sacks at the bottom of the route – a crack line that started as a shallow angled gully and steeped to a near vertical crack. I led the first pitch again, but either because it was wet and slippery or because I was nervous about the size of the route I was much less assured than the first day when I'd led the pitch easily. I managed to press on and was climbing reasonably well but was overcome by irrational waves of panic. I got to the hard move and clipped the peg. Because of the greasy rock I was taking more care to protect the pitch and I found a hole that I could thread with a wire sling that I hadn't used the previous time. This was my undoing, because having clipped this runner and then put a sling round a tree 3m higher there was much more rope drag than previously. Rather than make the next moves to the belay pegs I stopped at the tree and brought Muny up, apologising for not completing the pitch. This wasted some time since we have to swap round again on the peg belay so Muny could lead the following hard pitch as I didn't feel up to it. In part, although I didn't realise it at the time, my left hip was giving out, which meant I was unable to push up on my left knee and had to hop. I got a new hip five years later.

Meanwhile Scharlie was finding her way to the top of the mountain on the so-called M1. I watch Steve and Muny until they get too small to see then set off, my track taking me through thorny bushes, skirting round under the cliffs about half a mile before diving up a gully due north. Route finding was difficult because the red dots were sparse and faded. At one time I am following what I think are plentiful red dots until I realise they are red lichen. I scramble across slabs and ridges and through little gaps in the pinnacle rocks. In improbable places amongst the stone and scree tiny scented cyclamen and pale lilac autumn crocus splash the rock with colour. The dog accompanied me for the first half an hour then sensibly went back – he would have been a worry to me. I kept looking back to learn the route by fixing trees and rocks in my mind. Several times I thought if the way is not clear when I reach that ridge I'll stop, but there was always a cairn in the nick of time to encourage me.

On a narrow ledge I found a cave. The most punishing bit was a steeper loose scree slope that took an hour to climb. I set myself the goal of reaching the top at 2.30 but at 2.15 it was clear I was on the correct route and the path swung to the right, which meant I was in the home straight. I stood on the summit at 3.30 and ate my lunch. The view was panoramic and wonderful.

A cairn on Scharlie's walk up the mountain

Well near the top of the mountain

Goats on Scharlie's long walk

View from the top of the mountain

Below me there was a little flat field with a herd of goats and a well.

Back on our climb the rock was steeper and I had to concentrate on just the next move and look only for the next few feet rather than think about the route as a whole or look down at our increasing distance from the ground. The higher we got and the more I climbed the better I felt and by the third pitch, which was supposed to be the hardest, I found I was feeling more relaxed. We left the crack for the right wall and although it was steeper I didn't find it hard. There were plenty of holds and I could largely avoid the wet footholds. We got to a tree belay where the route diverged into a series of variations. The obvious line above us ran into vertical overhangs and the guide showed the route moving rightwards.

Muny led off again around the arête. There was one difficult move to get established and reach easier ground. When it came to my turn, I suspect I might have missed a hold or gone too high, but I got round and joined Muny again. I was climbing quickly and despite one or two nuts being difficult to get out had no real problems and was feeling good. The last pitch and the scramble to the summit were easy.

Muny suggested we try and abseil down Africana, the massive grey wall to our left, rather than descend the path and abseil down the route they'd used in the dark. That way we would be near our sacks and it would be more interesting. We followed the red dots upwards until we saw a letter "A" on the rock with an arrow pointing to the edge. Muny prospected down, trying

Panoram of Varasova showing how far Scharlie had to climb to reach the top of the mountain

to find the abseil and finally we decided to descend from a tree. As he was abseiling he saw he'd missed two bolts with shackles further to our right.

We were worried that the ropes might catch as we pulled them down becasue the way we gone was much more vegetated than if we gone from the bolts. We found the next belay, a tree, that was wreathed in old slings. The question was would the ropes pull down through the herbage. Luckily they did and we set off again. After what seemed an age Muny shouted to come. I'd been watching streams of lorries tipping gravel on the waterfront, possibly to extend the promenade, which seem to finish rather abruptly. What with the sound of their engines, the tipping gravel and the clamour of the horns I couldn't hear Muny's instructions. I decided that he must mean me to flip the rope round, since I was much further sideways than the ropes ran.

I started down. It was overhanging and below there was a sweep of 800 feet of grey wall. I concentrated on not dropping the descender and stripping the gear methodically – always setting up the abseil before unclipping my belay anchor. And then, trusting the rope and bolts and having double-checked that the descender was clipped correctly on the ropes and running free, I set off. Abseils like this need two things – method and lack of imagination.

Muny was still a way to my right and so I had to push over towards him with my feet. Finally I saw him. He was hanging from a single bolt on a featureless bit wall and to reach him I had to use a toe hook round a flake and reach out almost horizontally to the bolt before I slid past him. There was hardly anywhere to perch so I clipped the bolt and hung on in my harness. If you

didn't think about the exposure it was quite comfortable.

Now we had to hope that the ropes would pull down. They were not in a direct line and there were lots of places they could jam. There were small tough bushes and lots of excretions in the limestone, which the rope could catch on. I could see Muny was worried. It wouldn't be nice to be stuck up here hanging onto bolts on a grade too hard to climb. No doubt Rose and Neil would come and help us but they might not see us until it got dark, by which time we would be in for a real epic.

The first rope came down and we had the knot but my rope seemed to hang. Muny said we needed a knife and I assumed it must be jammed and he intended cutting it. But then he said he hadn't pulled hard yet and did so and it freed and ran easily slipping down the face with the slithering, hissing sound

Sheep on the ridge as Scharlie nears the top

that is such a relief to any climber in such a position.

We put in a friend as a last resort in case the bolt failed since Muny had spotted that the main abseil line was even further rightwards. He tied to one end of the rope and using the bots for aid climbed up to another bolt higher up and swung across to the slings on a rusty old karabiner. He took in the rope until he reached the knot and I threw him the other end so he would set up the next belay without untying the knot joining the two ropes. By the time he was ready to bring me up I had already reached down and collected the friend and had stripped the gear from the first bolt. I found the moves across surprisingly easy but nevertheless clipped in with some relief that we were now on the main abseil line.

We set up the next abseil and continued descending down the huge grey wall. There were four more long abseils to the bottom – all from good bolts. I descended slowly noting the route and assessing the moves and whether I felt I could make them. I had regained my climbing composure and was feeling good. Some of it looked quite reasonable but there were some blank stretches. It was well bolted, however, and would be a safe route to do, both because it was well protected and because one could abseil from any of the bolts. I was good at slab climbing and felt I could do it technically, but the face is huge and intimidating and looking up the steep slabs seemed to go on and on forever. It's such a long time since I've been on a big route that my eye and brain have become completely unaccustomed to this scale climbing. I tried to imagine how I would feel if I was starting out on it and leading from the bottom and realised I would be scared. The 5m high cliff behind Leveret croft is inadequate training for this scale of seriousness.

As we neared the bottom I became increasingly anxious about Scharlie. It was already dusk and I'd expected her to be down by now. On the mountain side it had taken Scharlie four and half hours to get up so she legged it down as fast as she could. She had a bad few minutes on the scree slope wondering if she'd missed the turn to the left, but the cairn she was looking for turned up. After that it was straightforward if tiring and she kept going strongly making sure she didn't trip and twist an ankle or worse.

At the bottom of the climb Steve packed his sack quickly and checked the time. It was well after five and would get dark at six. We decided to go back to the apartment as quickly as possible and ring her on the mobile. The not so faithful hound met us on the road as we climbed the stairs to the apartment with tired legs. I wondered if I would have the strength to go out on a search party or if I would just be a liability on my unsteady pins in the dark without a head torch. I needed to have a bite to eat and we needed to organise ourselves rather than just rush out in a panic.

On the balcony, using Muny's mobile I rang my own mobile and after what seemed an age of crackling Scharlie's voice answered and she said she was nearly down. She said she was below our route and waving a white handkerchief. Finally we spotted her – what a relief. And then she was coming down the road with the dog, scratched and tired but back safe. It was 5.45 and only 10 minutes or so from sunset. Steve was relieved that he didn't have to mount a search party. We called Rose and she said they were just abseiling down and would be back soon. She was making a habit of these late finishes. At least she knew the way the way down this time.

The sun was just setting over the sea to our right with crescent moon rising on the left when Muny, Steve and Scharlie went for a swim. The salt water was soothing for my cuts and bruises. Later we went back to Florence's restaurant and had much more food than we needed or wanted – a strange combination of Greek and Filipino cuisine that left us feeling rather queasy. We took the remains of the kebabs and rice back for breakfast.

Scharlie looking down on the Temple of Apollo, Delphi

Saturday 31 October

Scharlie and I wanted to visit Delphi on the way home so decided not to climb. Muny and Neil fix on a climb and Rose thought she'd done enough and would come with us to Delphi. We set off soon after ten and made good speed. The road was much better than we'd expected and we got to Delphi without much trouble about lunchtime. We bought tickets and then went to find the cafe that was further down the road. The situation was superb on a terrace overlooking the gorge under olive trees, but the coffee was Nescafé and Rose was disgusted.

Delphi is huge and full of interest. The only catch is that the temple of Apollo, the theatre and the stadium terraces are roped off; all the places you'd really like to go. Still it was fascinating. We measured the stadium and found it was 440 paces, the same size, although longer and narrower, as a modern stadium. Rose and Scharlie ran it while I snapped them. Rose particularly wanted a photo of herself next to the Sibylline rock. The museum was equally good and the few items on display the cream of the collection – the charioteer, the bull, the dish of Apollo and the marble youth. One could see how the Renaissance sculptors must have been inspired.

We reached Athens and uneventfully and met up with Tony. The hotel was

Scharlie 'on her marks' in the stadium at Delphi

Temple of Apollo, Delphi

Spartan but adequate and that evening we went out to a delightful restaurant called Hellenista that Tony booked for us. After dinner, despite the lateness of the hour and having to get to the airport by six, we drove to Lycabettus and climbed up to the church on the summit to get a view of the Acropolis. Tony pointed out the site of the new Olympic stadium and Hadrian's Gate. He also explained that Athens had been virtually deserted for over 1000 years from about 500 A.D. when Justinian closed the philosophy schools and turned terminal decline into final collapse. The city didn't become the capital until 1837 and Greek independence. This largely explains why so little of the ancient city remains today. Thessaloniki was a much more important centre throughout the Middle Ages and right up until the 19th century.

Sunday 1 November

An early start writing postcards and a last-minute dash to board and we're on our way home.

Acropolis from Lycabettus

Skoupa 5+ Varasova West face 200m 1966 by P. Idosidis - T. Zaharanis - M. Kottaris.

Views of Varasova

The Place of the Cold Waters (a Greek Ode)

O Varassova, where the mountain meets the sea!
Grey rock, black with rain, slicing into the plain
Cypress like brush-strokes, olive trees
The marshes, waved with reeds and cotton plants
Stretch to Missolonghi
Where heroes, long-forgotten, perished in cannonfire.

O Varassova, sun-warmed rock
Grey, grippy, steep; planted with thorns
We tie our ropes to stunted olive trees
To Turkey Oaks, bandaged with nylon slings
Where someone once gave up and headed home.
The sun goes down beyond Ithaca,
The black horizon of the middle sea.

O Varassova, coming home
Two strands of rope in the darkness
Headlamped like cavers
Every word shouted in the night
Heard by the barking dogs of the town
Farmers and fishermen sat in the bar
A child called indoors for playing late
No twilight but sudden dark.

O Varassova, place of the cold waters
Springs flow under the rock,
Stirring the warm sea
The gentle gulf
The dark deep salt sea depths
East towards Lepanto, Itea, Akrocorinth

O Varassova, landmark for the ships
Coming from Italy, Africa or Spain
Wars long-ended
Ships sunk in the cold clear sea.
We tempt danger by climbing the rock
Forgetting that elsewhere in the Middle Sea
Danger needs no temptation.

Poem by Rose Scott   16 November 2003

www.ingramcontent.com/pod-product-compliance
Lightning Source LLC
LaVergne TN
LVHW052301100826
845147LV00001B/114

* 9 7 8 1 9 1 2 4 6 0 2 1 2 *